I0158821

Copyright: © 2016 by Justin Imel

All rights reserved. No part of this publication may be reproduced, stored in a retrieval system, or transmitted in any form or by any means without prior written permission of the author. The only exception is brief quotations in printed reviews.

Published in The United States of America
By Dr. Justin Imel, Roanoke, VA

Manufactured in The United States of America
First edition published 2016
Cover art and jacket design © 2016 Justin Imel

Author photo – Shawn Sprouse, SDS Photography, Roanoke, VA

Scripture quotations are from the ESV® Bible (The Holy Bible, English Standard Version®), copyright © 2001 by Crossway, a publishing ministry of Good News Publishers. Used by permission. All rights reserved.

Revealing Revelation's Date

Dr. Justin Imel, Sr.

RJ&WC
Press

Dedication

This book is most affectionately dedicated to my friend and brother, Tommy Blewett. Tommy does a fine job in his preaching and teaching. In teaching Revelation, Tommy has advocated a late date. Although I believe Tommy is wrong, he has done a marvelous job with the difficult book.

Table of Contents

Statement of the Problem

Scholars date the New Testament Apocalypse at various times. Many scholars favor dating the work during the time of Domitian, while others argue for a Neronic date. Neither side possesses absolutely convincing support. Where one places the work affects his exegesis. For example, does the persecution involve imperial persecution or refer to localized tribulation during the Year of the Four Emperors and the wars which followed? One largely answers such questions based upon when he believes John wrote Revelation

This short work examines the writings of modern scholars relative to the dating of Revelation. These writings receive careful scrutiny. This analysis looks for faulty reasoning as well as an examination of the international evidence in Revelation itself. From Revelation's internal evidence, certain deductions can be made. From that evidence, I reject a composition during the reign of Domitian and argue for a writing during the reign of Galba.

Evidence of a Domitianic Date

As already stated, most scholars accept Revelation as a product of Domitian's reign. These scholars argue for a Domitianic date for a variety of reasons; however, most embrace the testimony of Church Fathers, especially the witness of Ireneaus.[1] Ireneaus served as bishop of

---

[1] For example, George Raymond Beasley-Murray, *The Book of Revelation*, New Century Bible Commentary (Grand Rapids: William B. Eerdmans Publishing Co., 1981), 37; D. A. Carson, Douglas J. Moo, and Leon Morris, *An Introduction to the New Testament* (Grand Rapids: Zondervan Publishing House, 1992), 473; Robert Henry Charles, *The Revelation of St. John*, The International Critical Commentary, vol. 1 (New York: Charles Scribner's Sons, 1920), xcii; Adela Yarbro Collins, "Dating the Apocalypse of John" *Biblical*

Lyons between AD175-190; he was a disciple of Polycarp, who himself was a disciple of the Apostle John. In *Against Heresies*, Ireneaus wrote, "For that [John's vision] was seen not very long since, but almost in our day, towards the end of Domitian's reign."[2] Eusebius quoted Ireneaus in his *Ecclesiastical History* and accepted a Domitianic date.[3] Many other ancient writers accepted a Domitianic date. However, many of these writers may have just been following Ireneaus when they attributed the book to the end of Domitian's reign.[4]

Yet, one can question Ireneaus'

Research 26 (1981): 33-34; Odis Duncan, "Bound But Released?" (Term Paper, Southern Christian University, 1996), 9; Homer Hailey, *Revelation: An Introduction and Commentary* (Grand Rapids: Baer Book House, 1979), 31; William Hendricksen, *More Than Conquerors* (Grand Rapids: Baker Book House, 1967), 20; Werner Georg Kummel, *An Introduction to the New Testament*, trans. Hoard Clark Kee (Nashville: Abingdon Press, 1975), 466; Robert H. Mounce, *The Book of Revelation* (Grand Rapids: William B. Eerdmans Publishing Co., 1977), 32; Ray Summers, *Worthy is the Lamb* (Nashville: Broadman Press, 1951), 83; and Henry Barclay Swete, *Commentary on Revelation* (London: Macmillan, 1911; reprint, Grand Rapids: Kregel Publications, 1977), xcix.

[2] Ireneaus *Against Heresies* 5.30.3.

[3] Eusebius *Ecclesiastical History* 3.18.

[4] Robert B. Moberly, "When Was Revelation Conceived?," *Biblica* 73 (1992): 381.

reliability. No extant copies of *Against Heresies* in Greek exist; only late Latin copies exist. Ireneaus was admittedly a small child when he received this information and did not write anything down for nearly 50 years.[5] Ireneaus does not serve as a credible witness.[6]

Revelation's author may have referred to a belief that Nero had not really died. Nero committed suicide in AD 68, but many Romans refused to believe such reports. Instead, many citizens believed Nero escaped to Parthia where he was actively preparing an army which would avenge his enemies.[7] In Revelation, John described the beast as having a mortal wound which had been healed.[8] John even described the beast as one who "was, and is not, and is about to

---

[5] Ibid.

[6] Barclay Newman critiques Ireneaus on the basis of his interpretation of the Apocalypse. Newman rejects Ireneaus because Ireneaus does not connect the Domitianic persecution with Revelation and because Ireneaus uses an allegorical approach to the book. See, Barclay Newman, "The Fallacy of the Domitian Hypothesis," *New Testament Studies* 10 (October 1963): 133-39.

[7] Paul S. Miner, "The Wounded Beast," *Journal of Biblical Literature* 72 (June 1953): 95; and Paul Trudinger, "The 'Nero Redivivus' Rumor and the Date of the Apocalypse of John," *Saint Mark's Review* 131 (September 1987): 43-44.

[8] Revelation 13:3, 12, 14.

rise from the bottomless pit."[9] Scholars generally argue this tradition took several years to develop, requiring a date in the nineties.[10]

However, one need not accept this explanation. According to Tacitus, no one took the Nero myth seriously by the reign of Domitian.[11] One arose in AD 69, and Tacitus says that the myth "threw Asia and Achaea into an uproar."[12] If John did intend to draw attention to a Nero myth, he could not easily have done so by the end of the first century.

Scholars also point to the condition of the churches in Revelation 2-3 as proof of a late date. Jesus described the church at Ephesus, Sardis,

---

[9] Revelation 17:8.

[10] Charles, xcv; Leon Morris, *The Book of Revelation*, rev. ed., Tyndale new Testament Commentaries (Grand Rapids: Eerdmans Publishing Co., 1987), 38; and Swete, ci-cii.

[11] Tacitus, *Histories* 1.2; and Donald Guthrie, *New Testament Introduction* (Downers Grove, IL: Inter-Varsity Press, 1970), 954.

[12] Tacitus *Histories* 3.1. See also John A. T. Robinson, *Redating the New Testament* (Philadelphia: The Westminster Press,1976), 245-46; Joseph Newbould Sanders, "St. John on Patmos," *New Testament Studies* 9 (January 1963): 77-78; and J. Christian Wilson, "The Problem of the Domitianic Date of Revelation," *New Testament Studies* 39 (October 1993): 598-99. See also, John M. Lawrence, "Nero Redivivus," *Fides et Historia* 11 (1978): 54-65 for a discussion of literature concerning the Nero myth.

and Laodicea as lacking in spiritual matters; writers often believe such a decline would have taken several years. Mounce says, "The spiritual decline at Ephesus, Sardis, and Laodicea would require an extended period of time."[13]

However, the Galatian churches declined quite rapidly. Paul told them, "I am astonished that you are so quickly deserting him who called you in the grace of Christ and are turning to a different gospel."[14] Paul could not believe that churches which at one time had been faithful quickly turned from their dedication. Since these churches declined rapidly, the Asian churches could also have declined rapidly.

Christ commended the Ephesians because that church "[hated] the works of the Nicolaitans"[15] which Christ also hated. Christ condemned the church at Pergamum because some disciples there held "the teaching of the Nicolaitans."[16] Since this group does not appear elsewhere in the new Testament, scholars postulate the group must have come into existence after the 60s.[17] Therefore, these scholars affirm, Revelation must have been dated

---

[13] Mounce, 34.
[14] Galatians 1:6.
[15] Revelation 2:6.
[16] Revelation 2:15.
[17] Mounce, 34; and Swete, ci.

in Domitian's day.

However, the teachings of the Nicolaitans were common in the 50s. This group taught that one could eat meat sacrificed to idols and could practice sexual immorality.[18] The Jerusalem Council (ad 51) centered around such teaching. 2 Peter (AD 64-66) deals with teachings similar to those of the Nicolaitans. The Nicolaitans, therefore, could well have existed prior to AD 96.

Christ told the church at Laodicea, "You say, I am rich, I have prospered, and I need nothing."[19] Such a statement shows the Laodiceans' dependence on wealth. An earthquake destroyed Laodicea in AD 60-61, and many writers maintain that the church could not be described as rich just a few years later.[20]

Yet, this view overlooks some important information. Tacitus said that Laodicea recovered from the earthquake with help from Rome.[21] Certainly, if Laodicea rebuilt herself after the earthquake, the city could have been prosperous just a few years later. Laodicea's rapid recovery might have given the church even more reason to

---

[18] Revelation 2:14-15.
[19] Revelation 3:17.
[20] Duncan, 9; Morris, 38; and Mounce, 35.
[21] Tacitus *The Annals of Imperial Rome* 14.27.

boast about their wealth.

In writing to the Philippians, Polycarp, a member of the church in Smyrna, stated that Paul "boasteth of you in all those churches which alone at that time knew God; for we know him not as yet."[22] Some accept Polycarp's statements that those churches "alone at that time knew God" to mean that the church in Smyrna did not exist in the 60s.[23] However, the statement from Polycarp only requires the church in Philippi to exist before the church in Smyrna, a fact attested in the New Testament.[24]

Reading through Revelation, one quickly learns the beast demanded worship. People worshiped the beast, and the image of the beast caused those who refused to worship the beast to be killed. God promised wrath on those who worshiped the beast. When the first angel poured out his bowl, a painful sore came upon all those who paid homage to the beast. A false prophet performed signs in order to deceive the beast's worshipers. Those who were slain because they had not worshiped the beast came to life and

---

[22] Polycarp *Epistle to the Romans* 11:3.

[23] For example, Charles, xciv; and Morris, 38.

[24] Kenneth Gentry, *The Beast of Revelation* (Tyler, TX: Institute for Christian Economics, 1989), 178-79; and Robinson, 229-30; see also, Guthrie, 955.

reigned with Christ a thousand years.[25]

Such language causes many to date Revelation during the reign of Domitian. Domitian jealously guarded his divine honors. During Domitian's reign, refusing to worship the emperor allowed one to be punished. Domitian not only wanted to be considered divine; he required worship.[26]

Although Rome honored Domitian with divinity, the imperial cult began long before Domitian's reign. Julius Caesar received divine worship.[27] Caligula required Romans to worship him.[28] According to Tacitus, a statue of Nero the same size as the one of Mars was set up in Rome in AD 55.[29] Even in Nero's time, the imperial cult firmly existed.

A cursory reading of Revelation shows the persecution the Asian churches faced. John identified himself as one who shared with the church in "the tribulation." Although the devil would throw some of them into prison, the Christians in Smyrna should not be afraid. Pergamum had lost Antipas, a faithful member,

---

[25] Revelation 13:3, 15; 14:9-11; 16:2; 19:20; 20:4.
[26] Guthrie, 950; Morris, 35-36; Mounce, 33; and Swete, ci.
[27] Guthrie, 949; and Mounce, 32.
[28] Mounce, 23.
[29] Tacitus *Annals of Imperial Rome* 13.8.

to martyrdom. Christ would keep the church at Philadelphia "from the hour of trial that [was] coming on the whole world." When the Lamb opened the fifth seal, John saw the souls of martyrs. The great harlot became drunk with the blood of the saints.[30]

Advocates of the late date theory claim such persecution could have only taken place during the reign of Domitian. For example, Ray Summers wrote, "The persecution of the Christian which is reflected in the book fits the Domitianic period alone."[31] Domitian was the second emperor after Nero to persecute the church.[32] Domitian had his kinsman Flavius put to death and banished Clemens' wife for "atheism." From cemetery inscriptions Clemens' wife Domitilla is believed to have been a Christian.[33] Clement of Rome speaks of "sudden and repeated misfortunes and calamities."[34] Since most scholars date Clement during the Domitianic period, many see this as a reference to persecutions under Domitian.[35]

The reference from Clement provides no

---

[30] Revelation 1:9; 2:10; 2:13; 3:10; 6:9; 17:6; 18:24; 19:2.
[31] Summers, 83.
[32] Kummel, 467.
[33] Guthrie, 952-53; Kummel, 467; and Mounce, 34.
[34] *Clement* 1.1.
[35] Guthrie, 952; and Mounce, 34.

evidence for dating Revelation in the nineties. Clement may or may not have spoken of persecution. "Sudden and repeated misfortunes and calamities" could refer to any number of events. Also, some evidence suggests that Clement may have written his epistle earlier than the traditional date.[36]

Domitian's killing of Clemens and banishment of Domitilla does not prove John wrote Revelation under Domitian. Dio Cassius wrote that Domitian took these actions for Clemens' atheism and "Jewish manners."[37] Dio Cassius lived late enough that he would have known the differences between Judaism and Christianity; Domitilla may not have been a Christian but a Jew.[38] In addition, one needs to remember that Dio Cassius showed hostility to Christianity. Had he known that Domitian persecuted Flavius Clemens and his wife for Christianity, one must wonder why the historian failed to mention that connection.[39] The cemetery inscriptions to which some scholars refer date

[36] See, Gentry, 123-27.

[37] Robinson, 323.

[38] Albert A. Bell, Jr., "The Date of John's Apocalypse: The Evidence of Some Roman Historians Reconsidered," *New Testament Studies* 25 (October 1978): 94.

[39] Duane Warden, "Imperial Persecution and the Dating of 1 Peter and Revelation," *Journal of the Evangelical Theological Society* 34 (June 1991): 206.

from the second century, not the first.[40]

Scholars should also note that most of the persecution discussed in Revelation lies in the future. John did identify himself as sharing in the "tribulation." Antipas had been martyred. But, the other references to persecution lie in the future. Antipas could easily have been killed by a local attack on Christians, something similar to the stoning of Stephen and the persecution in which Saul participated. Since Patmos served as a penal settlement, Rome obviously had John exiled there.[41] However, such banishment could have taken place at the request of the Jews or other groups. The Jews encouraged Roman authorities to jail Paul and Silas in Philippi.[42] These events occurred before Nero's reign.

Some also point to the similarities between Revelation and the Gospels of Matthew and Luke as pointing to a late date.[43] Since most scholars date Matthew and Luke in the 80s, Revelation is seen as a product of a later time.[44] However, the dating of the Gospels may not be correct; some scholars favor a date in the 60s.[45]

---

[40] Bell: 96.

[41] Gentry, 48.

[42] Acts 16:19ff.

[43] Charles, lxxxiii; and Guthrie 956.

[44] Guthrie, 956.

[45] Carson, Moo, and Morris, 76-79; and Coy Roper, *Notes on the New Testament* (Florence, AL:

Too, the similarities could be explained by John's being an eyewitness to Jesus.[46]

Next, let's take a look at the evidence for a Neronic date.

International Bible College, 1995), 22, 33.
[46] See, Guthrie, 956.

Evidence of a Neronic Date

Although most ancient authorities assign Revelation's composition to the reign of Domitian, some ancient writers ascribe the work to Nero's reign. Both Syriac versions of Revelation and Theophylact consider the work to come from the time of Nero.[1] Although these sources do not hold the credibility of Ireneaus or Eusebius, they do illustrate that even in antiquity a late date was not always accepted.

Revelation 17 plays an important role in understanding when John wrote the book. John wrote, "This calls for a mind with wisdom: the

---

[1] Charles, xcii. See Gentry, 138-48 for a list of other external evidence for an early date for Revelation.

seven heads are seven mountains on which the woman is seated; they are also seven kings, five of whom have fallen, one is, the other has not yet come, and when he does come he must remain only a little while."[2] If one can arrive at an understanding of which five kings have fallen, he can know when Revelation was written.

However, such an understanding does not come about easily. Scholars do not agree on which emperor should begin the list. Some begin with Julius Caesar, and others begin with Augustus. Some even begin with Caligula, the first emperor to receive divine honors for himself.[3] Some also insist one should only could those who were deified by the Senate; such calculations would omit Nero and make Titus the fifth emperor.[4] Others do not see literal emperors in view; Mounce, for example, sees the kings as being symbolic for the power of the Roman Empire.[5]

Evidence causes several scholars to regard Julius Caesar as the first Roman emperor. Suetonius begins his list of emperors with Caesar.[6] Caesar wore the title "imperator" and

---

[2] Revelation 17:9-10.

[3] Bell: 97; and Collins: 36.

[4] Bell: 97.

[5] Mounce, 315-16.

[6] Gentry, 107; and Wilson: 599.

was emperor *de facto*.[7] Dio Cassius also counts Julius as the first Roman emperor in *Roman History*.[8] Moreover, certain Jewish and Christian pseudepigraphical works consider Caesar the first Roman emperor. The *Sibylline Oracles* consider Caesar the first Roman emperor.[9] *Second Esdras* and the *Epistle of Barnabas* follow suit.[10]

However, Tacitus regarded Augustus as the first emperor,[11] and apparently John followed him. In Revelation 13, John saw a vision of a beast rising out of the sea. One of the beast's heads seemed to have a fatal wound, but that wound had been healed.[12] This appears to be a reference to Nero's wound from his suicide and indicates John wrote Revelation after Nero's death. In that case, the first emperor cannot be Julius Caesar, for such calculations would make Nero the king "who is."

Scholars greatly argue whether or not Galba, Otho, and Vitellius should be considered Roman emperors. Rejection comes because confusion existed among the Roman people; the Romans were not sure whether or not they should accept them. Also, all three of these emperors

---

[7] Robinson, 243.
[8] Gentry, 107.
[9] *Sibylline Oracles* 5.12-15.
[10] *Second Esdras* 12.15; and *Epistle of Barnabas* 4.4.
[11] Wilson: 599.
[12] Revelation 13:3, 12.

served a short term.

However, no compelling evidence exists for rejecting these three as rightful Roman emperors. Although Suetonius spoke of them as "rebellious princes," he included these three in his *Lives of the Twelve Caesars*. Tacitus and Josephus place them among the other emperors.[13] That these three reigned for such a short period of time should not deter one from considering them emperors.[14]

Revelation 13:18 points to Nero was the beast of Revelation. That text reads: "This calls for wisdom: let the one who has understanding calculate the number of the beast, for it is the number of a man, and his number is 666." When Nero's title is placed in Hebrew characters, the number comes to 666.[15] A textual variant also arose which gives the number of the beast as 616; this variant may have arisen because Nero's title in Latin would have that numerical value.[16]

---

[13] Robinson, 243.

[14] Collins: 36.

[15] David A. DeSilva, "The Social Setting of the Revelation to John: Conflicts Within, Fears Wtihout," *Westminster Theological Journal* 54 (Fall 1992): 275; Gentry, 33-34; Lawrence: 54-55; and W. B. West, Jr., *Revelation Through First-Century Glasses* (Nashville: Gospel Advocate Company, 1997, 96-97.

[16] Gentry, 34-36; and Bruce M. Metzger, *A Textual Commentary on the Greek New Testament* (Stuttgart:

Revelation also seems to have been written prior to the destruction of the temple in Jerusalem. John was told to measure the temple, the altar, and those who worshiped there; he was not to measure the outside court for that court would be given to the nations who would trample the holy city for forty-two months.[17] The nations (or Gentiles) took not only the outer court but took the entire temple in Jerusalem's destruction in AD 70. John intended to use forty-two months as a period where evil reigns, not a literal period of time.[18] Although certain scholars contend the temple should not be taken literally,[19] the prophecy seems to deal with the destruction of Jerusalem.[20]

The passage should be seen as a prophecy concerning the destruction of Jerusalem for two reasons. First, John clearly intends to portray literal Jerusalem as the city under discussion. He calls the city the "holy city" and says that the

---

United Bible Societies, 1975), 750.

[17] Revelation 11:1-2.

[18] Robinson: 239. Wilson, who uses this text to argue for a pre-AD 70 composition, argues that the seer made a mistake in predicting an occupation lasting forty-two months; Wilson: 604.

[19] For example, Guthrie, 960.

[20] Some commentators believe this section was written by a zealot prior to AD 70 and then incorporated into Revelation sometime later. See, Collins: 37-38; and Mounce, 218-19.

Lord was crucified in the city.[21] This would rule out seeing the city as heaven or Rome. Second, a tenth of the city fell.[22] The city fell as part of God's judgment as indicated by John's calling the earthquake the "second woe."[23] John portrayed God as bringing judgment on Rome, an event which occurred in AD 70.

---

[21] Revelation 11:2, 8.

[22] Revelation 11:13.

[23] Revelation 11:14; see Gentry, 123-27 for a discussion of Clement's speaking of the temple in the present tense.

Conclusion

Although modern scholarship often sees Revelation's composition as occurring under Domitian, the evidence points in another direction. Ireneaus' statement in *Against Heresies* proves little. Since men arose claiming to be Nero shortly after his suicide, the Nero redivivus myth probably did not take 30 years to develop. The spiritual stagnation of the Asian churches does not require a lengthy period. The imperial cult existed even before Nero's reign. No compelling evidence exists for seeing Domitian as a harsh persecutor of Christianity. The similarities between Revelation and two of the Synoptics does not push Revelation's composition into the last decade of the first century.

John probably wrote the Apocalypse shortly after the death of Nero, during the reign of Galba. A few ancient writers point toward this date as does the list of kings in Revelation 17. No credible excuse exists for excluding Galba, Otho, and Vitellius from the list of Roman emperors. Nero could very well be the beast portrayed in Revelation. John even foretold the destruction of the temple in Jerusalem, an even which occurred in AD 70.

Modern scholars would do well to reconsider the evidence concerning the dating of Revelation. Simply parroting what others scholars have written will not suffice. A careful scrutiny of modern writings provides no real evidence for accepting a late date except that the date is "traditional." The tradition does not account for the internal evidence in Revelation. The tradition, therefore, should be rejected in favor of a date during the reign of Galba.

Works Cited

Beasley-Murray, George Raymond. *The Book of Revelation*. New Century Bible Commentary. Grand Rapids: William B. Eerdmans Publishing Co., 1981.

Bell, Albert A. "The Date of John's Apocalypse: The Evidence of some Roman Historians Reconsidered." *New Testament Studies* 25 (October 1978): 93-102.

Carson, D. A., Douglas J. Moo, and Leon Morris. *An Introduction to the New Testament*. Grand Rapids: Zondervan Publishing House, 1992.

Charles, Robert Henry. *The Revelation of St. John*. Vol 1. The International Critical Commentary. New York: Charles

Scribner's Sons, 1920.

Collins, Adela Yarbro. "Dating the Apocalypse of John." *Biblical Research* 26 (1981): 33-44.

DeSilva, David A. "The social Setting of the Revelation to John: Conflicts Within, Fears Without." *Westminster Theological Journal* 54 (Fall 1992): 273-302.

Duncan, Odis. "Bound But Released?" Term Paper, Southern Christian University, 1996.

Epistle of Barnabas.

Eusebius. *Ecclesiastical History*.

Gentry, Kenneth. *The Beast of Revelation*. Tyler, TX: Institute for Christian Economics, 1989.

Guthrie, Donald. *New Testament Introduction*. Downers Grove, IL: Inter-Varsity Press, 1970.

Hailey, Homer. *Revelation: An Introduction and Commentary*. Grand Rapids: Baker Book House, 1979.

Hendricksen, William. *More Than Conquerors*. Grand Rapids: Baker Book House,

1967.

Ireneaus. *Against Heresies.*

Kummel, Werner George. *Introduction to the New Testament.* Translated by Howard Clark Kee. Nashville: Abingdon Press. 1975.

Lawrence, John M. "Nero Redivivus." *Fides et Historia* 11 (1978): 54-65.

Metzger, Bruce M. *A Textual Commentary on the Greek New Testament.* Stuttgart: United Bible Societies, 1975.

Miner, Paul S. "The Wounded Beast." *Journal of Biblical Literature* 72 (June 1953): 93-101.

Moberly, Robert B. "When Was Revelation Conceived?" *Biblica* 73 (1992): 373-93.

Morris, Leon. *Revelation*, rev. ed. Tyndale New Testament Commentaries. Grand Rapids: William B. Eerdmans Publishing Co., 1987.

Mounce, Robert H. *The Book of Revelation.* Grand Rapids: William B. Eerdmans Publishing Co., 1977.

Newman, Barclay. "The Fallacy of the Domitian Hypothesis." *New Testament Studies* 10

(October 1963): 133-39.

Polycarp. *Epistle to the Philippians.*

Robinson, John A. T. *Redating the New Testament.* Philadelphia: The Westminster Press, 1976.

Roper, Coy. *Notes on the New Testament.* Florence, AL: International Bible College, 1995.

Sanders, Joseph Newbould. "St. John on Patmos." *New Testament Studies* 9 (January 1963): 75-85.

Second Esdras.

Sibylline Oracles.

Summers, Ray. *Worthy Is the Lamb.* Nashville: Broadman Press, 1951.

Swete, Henry Barclay. *Commentary on Revelation.* London: Macmillan, 1911. Reprint, Grand Rapids: Kregel Publications, 1977.

Tacitus. *The Annals of Imperial Rome.*

_____. *Histories.*

Trudinger, Paul. "The 'Nero Redivivus' Rumor and the Date of the Apocalypse to

John." *Saint Mark's Review* 131 (September 1987): 43-44.

Warden, Duane. "Imperial Persecution and the Dating of 1 Peter and Revelation." *Journal of the Evangelical Theological Society* 34 (June 1991): 202-12.

West, Jr., W. B. *Revelation Through First-Century Glasses*. Nashville: Gospel Advocate Co., 1997.

Wilson, J. Christian. "The Problem of the Domitianic Date of Revelation." *New Testament Studies* 39 (October 1993): 587-605.

About the Author

Dr. Justin Imel is married to the former Tammy McKinney; the Imels have two children, RJ and Wilson. Dr. Imel has served churches of Christ in Kentucky, West Virginia, Tennessee, and Virginia. He has taught at Appalachian Bible Institute, Ohio Valley University, and Heritage Christian University. Dr. Imel holds a Doctor of Ministry in Church Leadership and Church Growth from Amridge University in Montgomery, Alabama. The Imels make their home in Roanoke, Virginia, with their puppy, Bacon.

Dr. Imel loves Alabama football, Kentucky basketball, and Indy Car racing. He enjoys writing, Starbucks, coin collecting, and history. He and his family are members of the Lake Drive church of Christ in Vinton, Virginia.

Also by the Author

Accompanied by the Instruments of David

Messages from the Manger

On Momma's Knee

Selected Sermons

Selfless Service

Shepherding Wandering Sheep

Thinking about John

Two Wonders

www.ingramcontent.com/pod-product-compliance
Lightning Source LLC
Chambersburg PA
CBHW060640030426
42337CB00018B/3411